To:

Samantha. Wishing you a
Wonderful Christmas ♥

From:

Kelli with gratefulness and
appreciation for all you do.

Christmas
TREASURES

The quoted ideas expressed in this book (but not Scripture verses) are not, in all cases, exact quotations, as some have been edited for clarity and brevity. In all cases, the author has attempted to maintain the speaker's original intent. In some cases, quoted material for this book was obtained from secondary sources, primarily print media. While every effort was made to ensure the accuracy of these sources, the accuracy cannot be guaranteed. For additions, deletions, corrections, or clarifications in future editions of this text, please write Brighton Books.

Cover design & page layout by: Bart Dawson
Copy written and compiled by: Criswell Freeman

ISBN 1-58334-207-9

1 2 3 4 5 6 7 8 9 10 • 03 04 05 06 07 08 09 10

Printed in the United States of America

Merry Christmas

Contents

It's Christmastime, and there is so much to do: meals to cook, parties to plan, and presents to wrap. Sometimes, amid the crush of holiday obligations, we may be tempted to forget, at least temporarily, the One whose birth we celebrate. But as Christians, our most important obligation is clear: We must thank our Heavenly Father and give praise for His ultimate gift: the Christ child.

This little book celebrates the treasures of Christmas, beginning, of course, with God's greatest treasure, His only begotten Son. Into humble circumstances God sent Jesus to become the source of joyful abundance and eternal salvation for believers of every generation. And now, as Christians who have received God's rich blessings, it is our turn to celebrate the birth of the baby Jesus.

The holiday season provides us with countless opportunities to gather together and offer thanks for God's love and for His blessings. How will you celebrate Christmas this year? Hopefully, you will make Christ the centerpiece of your holiday celebrations. When you do, you will encounter a multitude of spiritual treasures that will serve to enrich Christmas Day and every other day of the year.

A Child Is Born

But the angel said to them, "Do not be afraid, for you see,
I announce to you good news of great joy that will be for
all the people: because today in the city of David was born for you
a Savior, who is Christ the Lord.

Luke 2:10-11 HCSB

Christmas is the glorious day on which we celebrate that pivotal event in human history, the birth of Christ. No amount of commercialism or fanfare should obscure the fact that Christmastime is the annual birthday celebration for the Christian faith, a time for believers everywhere to rejoice, to pray, and to give thanks for God's greatest treasure: His Son.

Billy Graham observed, "Christmas is the celebration of the event that set Heaven to singing, an event that gave the stars of the night sky a new brilliance." As we prepare for the busy days that lead up to Christmas, it is appropriate that we remain mindful of the *real* reason for the holiday season by offering our prayers and our praise to the One whose birth we celebrate.

On Christmas Day two thousand years ago,
the birth of a tiny baby in an obscure village in the Middle East
was God's supreme triumph of good over evil.

Charles Colson

Jesus Christ was born into this world, not from it.

Oswald Chambers

At Bethlehem God became man to enable men
to become the sons of God.

C. S. Lewis

Christmas is about a baby, born in a stable,
who changed the world forever.

John Maxwell

Jesus Christ founded His Kingdom on the weakest link of all: a Baby.

Oswald Chambers

Tell me the story of Jesus. Write on my heart every word.
Tell me the story most precious, sweetest that ever was heard.

Fanny Crosby

See, the virgin will be with child
and give birth to a son, and they will name
Him Immanuel, which is translated
"God is with us."

—

Matthew 1:23 HCSB

What Child Is This

What child is this, Who, laid to rest,
on Mary's lap is sleeping?
Whom angels greet with anthems sweet,
while shepherds watch are keeping?

This, this is Christ the King,
Whom shepherds guard and angels sing. Haste,
haste to bring Him laud,
the Babe, the Son of Mary.

—

William C. Dix

You have come to us as a small child,
but you have brought us the greatest of
all gifts, the gift of eternal love.
Caress us with your tiny hands, embrace us
with your tiny arms, and pierce our hearts
with your soft, sweet cries.

—

Bernard of Clairvaux

*H*e was created of a mother whom he created. He was carried by hands that he formed. He cried in the manger in wordless infancy, he, the Word, without whom all human eloquence is mute.

—

Augustine of Hippo

The manger is a symbol of what can happen
when Jesus Christ resides inside us.

Bill Hybels

The crucial question for each of us is this:
What do you think of Jesus, and do you yet
have a personal acquaintance with Him?

Hannah Whitall Smith

Whoever believes that Jesus is the Christ is born of God,
and whoever loves the Father loves the child born of Him.

1 John 5:1 NASB

For a child is born to us, a son is given to us. And the government will rest on his shoulders. These will be his royal titles: Wonderful Counselor, Mighty God, Everlasting Father, Prince of Peace.

—

Isaiah 9:6 NLT

We tend to focus our attention at Christmas on the infancy of Christ. The greater truth of the holiday is His deity. More astonishing than a baby in the manger is the truth that this promised baby is the omnipotent Creator of the heavens and the earth!

John MacArthur

The King of kings and Lord of lords, the only Begotten of the Father was born in a stable, raised by a poor carpenter, teased by his brothers, and was virtually homeless, practically penniless. He was deserted by his friends, insulted in a kangaroo court, mocked, beaten, stripped, bruised, then crucified. To us it is a scenario that makes little sense. To God it was the only scenario that made any sense.

Beth Moore

God sent His light into a very dark world that first Christmas.
No longer would darkness reign because that little light would grow
to be a man who would take away the sin of the world.

Steve Russo

Therefore if any man be in Christ, he is a new creature:
old things are passed away; behold, all things are become new.

2 Corinthians 5:17 KJV

Go tell it on the mountain,
over the hills and everywhere.
Go tell it on the mountain,
that Jesus Christ is born!

—

Traditional Spiritual

A Season of Thanksgiving

Thanks be to God for His indescribable gift.

2 Corinthians 9:15 HCSB

During the Christmas season, we give thanks for the miraculous gifts that God has bestowed upon the world through His Son, Jesus Christ. But, thanksgiving should never be reserved for holidays or special occasions. To the contrary, we should offer thanksgiving and praise to our Creator many times each day.

God has blessed us in countless ways, and we owe Him everything, including our never-ending praise. May we honor Him and praise Him today, tomorrow, and throughout eternity.

Christmas is a good time
to take stock of our blessings.

—

Pat Boone

*I*t is good to give thanks to the LORD,
to sing praises to the Most High.

—

Psalm 92:1 HCSB

A child of God should be
a visible beatitude for happiness
and a living doxology for gratitude.

—

C. H. *Spurgeon*

It is only with gratitude that life becomes rich.

Dietrich Bonhoeffer

Thanksgiving or complaining—these words express two contrastive attitudes of the souls of God's children in regard to His dealings with them. The soul that gives thanks can find comfort in everything; the soul that complains can find comfort in nothing.

Hannah Whitall Smith

Christmas offers its wonderful message: Emmanuel—God with us.
He who resided in Heaven, co-equal and co-eternal
with the Father and the Spirit,
willingly descended into our world.

Charles Swindoll

No duty is more urgent than that of returning thanks.

St. Ambrose

God is worthy of our praise and is pleased when
we come before Him with thanksgiving.

Shirley Dobson

Enter his gates with thanksgiving; go into his courts with praise.
Give thanks to him and bless his name. For the Lord is good.
His unfailing love continues forever,
and his faithfulness continues to each generation.

Psalm 100:4-5 NLT

The words "thank" and "think"
come from the same root word.
If we would think more,
we would thank more.

—

Warren Wiersbe

*P*raise and thank God
for who He is and
for what He has done for you.

—

Billy Graham

Joy is the simplest form of gratitude.

Karl Barth

God has promised that if we harvest well with the tools of
thanksgiving, there will be seeds for planting in the spring.

Gloria Gaither

And let the peace of God rule in your hearts . . .
and be ye thankful.

Colossians 3:15 KJV

All praise to Thee, Eternal Lord, clothed in a garb
of flesh and blood, choosing a manger for a throne.

Martin Luther

Come, let us sing to the LORD! Let us give a joyous shout
to the rock of our salvation! Let us come before him
with thanksgiving. Let us sing him psalms of praise.

Psalm 95:1-2 NLT

Lord, the celebration of the birth of Jesus is joyous.
During this time of thanksgiving, keep me ever mindful
of Christ's life and of His sacrifice.

Jim Gallery

A spirit of thankfulness makes all the difference.

Billy Graham

Bless the LORD, O my soul, and forget not all his benefits.

Psalm 103:2 KJV

A Time for Sharing

The one who has two shirts must share with someone who has none,
and the one who has food must do the same.

Luke 3:11 HCSB

The thread of generosity is woven—completely and inextricably—into the very fabric of Christ's teachings. If we are to be disciples of Christ, we, too, must give freely of our time, our possessions, and our love.

During the Christmas season and throughout the year, we are called upon to be cheerful, generous, courageous givers. The world needs our help, but even more importantly, we need the spiritual rewards that God bestows upon us when we give cheerfully and without reservation.

Freely you have received, freely give.

Matthew 10:8 NIV

This is the essence of the Christmas story: a spirit of giving;
giving not from a sense of duty, not as a return for receiving,
but from an awareness that in a world where so much is given
to man, man, too, should himself give gifts.

Anne Bryan McCall

We must not only give what we have;
we must also give what we are.

Désiré Joseph Mercier

Christmas gift suggestions: to your enemy, forgiveness;
to an opponent, tolerance; to a friend, your heart;
to a customer, service; to all, charity;
to every child, a good example;
and to yourself, respect.

Oren Arnold

We have finally mastered the meaning of Christmas
when Christmas becomes a way of life.

Leo Buscaglia

*C*hristmas, my child, is love in action.
Every time we love, every time we give,
it's Christmas.

—

Dale Evans

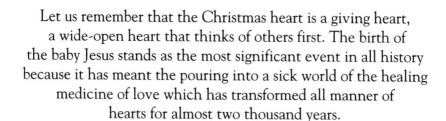

Let us remember that the Christmas heart is a giving heart,
a wide-open heart that thinks of others first. The birth of
the baby Jesus stands as the most significant event in all history
because it has meant the pouring into a sick world of the healing
medicine of love which has transformed all manner of
hearts for almost two thousand years.

George Matthew Adams

We are never more like God than when we give.

Charles Swindoll

Christmas is not a time nor a season, but a state of mind.
To cherish peace and goodwill, to be plenteous in mercy,
is to have the real spirit of Christmas.

Calvin Coolidge

Unless we make Christmas an occasion to share our blessings,
all the snow in Alaska won't make it "white."

Bing Crosby

To celebrate the heart of Christmas is to forget ourselves
in the service of others.

Henry C. Link

The Spirit of Christmas is the Light of the world.

Dorothy Walworth Crowell

If we have the true love of God in our hearts, we will show it
in our lives. We will not have to go up and down the earth
proclaiming it. We will show it in everything we say or do.

D. L. Moody

It is the duty of every Christian to be Christ to his neighbor.

Martin Luther

Christmas! 'Tis the season for kindling
the fire of hospitality in the hall,
the genial fire of charity in the heart.

—

Washington Irving

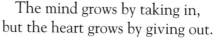

The mind grows by taking in,
but the heart grows by giving out.

Warren Wiersbe

The measure of a life, after all,
is not its duration but its donation.

Corrie ten Boom

Abundant living means abundant giving.

E. Stanley Jones

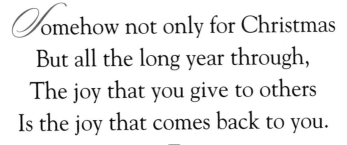

Somehow not only for Christmas
But all the long year through,
The joy that you give to others
Is the joy that comes back to you.

—

John Greenleaf Whittier

So let each one give as he purposes
in his heart, not grudgingly or of necessity;
for God loves a cheerful giver.

—

2 Corinthians 9:7 NKJV

Home for Christmas

He blesses the home of the righteous.

Proverbs 3:33 NIV

Few words in the English language are more reassuring than the familiar phrase: "Home for Christmas!" Christmas can be a time for sharing feelings of warmth and appreciation with those we love, and if we can share those feelings in person, we are truly blessed.

Let's resolve to make this Christmas a time to express our love and affection for those who keep the home fires burning. When we do, we make ourselves dutiful servants of the One whose birth is the reason for this glorious season.

Surely Christmas is the very best time
of the year to be home with loved ones.

—

W. Herschel Ford

Christmas is being together—gathering together.
It is the time of the heart's inventory.
It is the time of going home in many ways.

William Saroyan

And if our fellowship below in Jesus be so sweet,
what greater blessings shall we know
when 'round His throne we meet?

Charles Wesley

When the family is together on
Christmas day,
all is well with the world!

—

Marie T. Freeman

A Christmas family-party!
We know of nothing in nature
more delightful!

—

Charles Dickens

The first essential for a happy home is love.

Billy Graham

At Christmas all roads lead home.

Marjorie Holmes

How good and pleasant it is when brothers live together in unity!

Psalm 133:1 NIV

Being able to share with others gives Christmas its meaning.

Michael Landon

Gifts of time and love are surely the basic ingredients
of a truly merry Christmas.

Peg Bracken

Christmas is, of course, the time to be home—
in heart as well as body.

Garry Moore

*C*hristmas is a together time.

—

Charles Schulz

*T*he best gift of all:
the presence of a happy family
all wrapped up in one another.

—

Anonymous

The Treasured Songs of Christmas

Is anyone happy? Let him sing songs of praise.

James 5:13 NIV

Every year, as Christmas Day draws near, we are treated to the heartwarming sounds of our most treasured holiday hymns and carols. The songs of Christmas, especially our favorite hymns, rank among the most beloved compositions ever penned.

On the pages that follow, we celebrate a few of the beloved songs we sing at Christmastime. Enjoy!

What sweeter music can we bring
Than a carol for to sing
The birth of this our heavenly king.

—

Robert Herrick

Jingle Bells

Dashing thro' the snow in a one-horse open sleigh,
O'er the fields we go, laughing all the way;
Bells on bob-tail ring, making spirits bright;
What fun it is to ride and sing
a sleighing song tonight.

Jingle bells! Jingle bells! Jingle all the way!
Oh! what fun it is to ride in a one-horse open sleigh.

A day or two ago I thought I'd take a ride,
And soon Miss Fanny Bright was seated by my side;
The horse was lean and lank, misfortune seemed
his lot. He got into a drifted bank, and we,
we got upshot.

Jingle bells! Jingle bells! Jingle all the way!
Oh! what fun it is to ride in a one-horse open sleigh.

—

John Pierpoint, 1827

It Came Upon a Midnight Clear

It came upon the midnight clear,
That glorious song of old,
From angels bending near the earth,
To touch their harps of gold.
Peace on the earth, goodwill to men,
From Heaven's all gracious King,
The world in solemn stillness lay,
To hear the angels sing.

For lo! the days are hastening on,
By prophet-bards foretold,
When with the ever-circling years
Comes round the age of gold;
When peace shall over all the earth
Its ancient splendors fling,
And the whole world give back the song
Which now the angels sing.

—

Edmund Sears, 1850

Away in a Manger

Away in a manger, no crib for a bed,
The little Lord Jesus lay down his sweet head.
The stars in the sky looked down where he lay,
The little Lord Jesus, asleep on the hay.

The cattle are lowing, the baby awakes,
But little Lord Jesus, no crying he makes.
I love Thee, Lord Jesus!

Look down from the sky,
And stay by my cradle till morning is nigh.

Be near me, Lord Jesus, I ask Thee to stay
Close by me forever, and love me, I pray.
Bless all the dear children in thy tender care,
And fit us for heaven,
to live with Thee there.

—

Anonymous

O Little Town of Bethlehem

O little town of Bethlehem,
How still we see thee lie,
Above thy deep and dreamless sleep,
The silent stars go by;
Yet in thy dark streets shineth
The everlasting Light,
The hopes and fears of all the years
Are met in thee tonight.

O holy Child of Bethlehem!
Descend to us we pray;
Cast out our sin and enter in,
Be born in us today.
We hear the Christmas angels
The great glad tidings tell;
O come to us abide with us,
Our Lord Emmanuel!

—

Phillips Brooks, 1867

God Rest You Merry Gentlemen

God rest you merry, gentlemen,
Let nothing you dismay,
Remember Christ our Savior
Was born on Christmas Day,
To save us all from Satan's pow'r
When we were gone astray;
O tidings of comfort and joy, comfort and joy,
O tidings of comfort and joy.

From God our heavenly Father,
A blessed angel came.
And unto certain shepherds,
Brought tidings of the same;
How that in Bethlehem was born
The Son of God by name;
O tidings of comfort and joy, comfort and joy,
O tidings of comfort and joy.

—

Traditional 17th-Century English Carol

Silent Night

Silent Night! Holy Night!
All is calm, all is bright.
Round yon virgin mother and child!
Holy infant so tender and mild,
Sleep in heavenly peace,
sleep in heavenly peace.

Silent Night! Holy Night!
Shepherds quake at the sight!

Glories stream from heaven afar,
Heavenly hosts sing Alleluia
Christ the Savior is born! Christ the Savior is born!

Silent Night! Holy Night!
Son of God, love's pure light;
Radiant beams from Thy holy face,
with the dawn of redeeming grace,
Jesus Lord, at Thy birth, Jesus Lord, at Thy birth.

—

Father Joseph Mohr, 1818

O Come All Ye Faithful

O come, all ye faithful, joyful and triumphant,
O come ye, O come ye, to Bethlehem.
Come and behold him,
born the King of angels;

O come, let us adore him,
O come, let us adore him,
O come, let us adore him,
Christ the Lord.

Sing, choirs of angels, sing in exultation;
O sing, all ye citizens of heaven above!
Glory to God, all glory in the highest;

O come, let us adore him,
O come, let us adore him,
O come, let us adore him,
Christ the Lord.

—

John Francis Wade, 1742

Hark! The Herald Angels Sing

Hark! the herald angels sing,
"Glory to the newborn King. Peace on earth
and mercy mild; God and sinners reconciled."
Joyful all ye nations rise. Join the triumph of
the skies; with angelic host proclaim,
"Christ is born in Bethlehem!"
Hark! The herald angels sing,
"Glory to the newborn King."

—

Charles Wesley, 1739

Treasures
from the Heart

Let love and faithfulness never leave you . . .
write them on the tablet of your heart.

Proverbs 3:3 NIV

God is love, and the birthday celebration of God's Son is a time when love should fill our hearts. Christmas is a season for exchanging not only gifts but also feelings of warmth, appreciation, endearment, and fellowship.

As we gather together during this holiday season, let's make this Christmas a time to express genuine love and affection for our families and friends. When we do, we share the same priceless Christmas treasure that God first shared with us.

It is Christmas in the heart
that puts Christmas in the air.

—

W. T. Ellis

*L*ove came down at Christmas,
Love all lovely, Love Divine;
Love was born at Christmas;
Star and angels gave the sign.

—

Christina Rossetti

Selfishness makes Christmas a burden; love makes it a delight.

Anonymous

There is a love at Christmas because Christmas was born of love. Let us, each one, keep alive this spirit of love and glorify God.

Josepha Emms

We have the Lord, but He Himself has recognized that we need the touch of a human hand. He Himself came down and lived among us. We cannot see Him now, but blessed be the tie that binds human hearts in Christian love.

Vance Havner

May you have the gladness of Christmas which is hope;
the spirit of Christmas which is peace;
the heart of Christmas which is love.

Ada V. Hendricks

Christmas is not just a day of the year.
It is also—and more importantly— a condition of the heart.

Marie T. Freeman

There are all kinds of presents one can get for Christmas.
The best is love.

Helen Hayes

*N*ow these three remain:
faith, hope, and love.
But the greatest of these is love.

—

1 Corinthians 13:13 HCSB

Blessed is the season which engages
the whole world in a celebration of love.
Hamilton Wright Mabie

The Christmas spirit—love—changes hearts and lives.
Pat Boone

Carve your name on hearts, not on marble.
C. H. Spurgeon

He who is filled with love is filled with God Himself.
St. Augustine

Love one another earnestly from a pure heart.
1 Peter 1:22 HCSB

Love is an attribute of God.
To love others is evidence of a genuine faith.
Kay Arthur

*M*ay the Lord cause you to increase
and abound in love for one another,
and for all people.

—

1 Thessalonians 3:12 NASB

Treasured Memories

I thank my God every time I remember you.

Philippians 1:3 NIV

Holiday memories: Oh, how we treasure them! As December 25th approaches, we encounter a double dose of memory-evoking events: first, the passing of another Christmas, and then, only one week later, the passing of another year. No wonder we find ourselves reflecting on the past.

This year, as we make more holiday memories, let's pause to praise God for all His blessings: past, present, and future.

*O*ur hearts grow tender with childhood
memories and love of kindred,
and we are better throughout the year for
having, in spirit, become a child again
at Christmastime.

—

Laura Ingalls Wilder

Happy, happy Christmas, that can win us back to the delusions
of our childhood days, recall to the old man the pleasures of his youth,
and transport the traveler back to his own fireside and quiet home!

Charles Dickens

You remember hundreds of Christmas moments,
and you laugh—or weep—with the dearest of them.

Margaret Lee Runbeck

Christmas is a big love affair
to remove the wrinkles of the year
with kindly remembrances.

—

John Wanamaker

$\mathcal{C}$hristmas is the most evocative
and nostalgic day of the year.

—

Clare Boothe Luce

For children, Christmas is anticipation.
For adults, Christmas is memory.

Eric Sevareid

When we recall Christmas past, we usually find that
the simplest things—not the great occasions—
give off the greatest glow of happiness.

Bob Hope

*A*s another Christmas passes,
the memory of it stays and hovers like
the scent of cedar. And even if it can't be
Christmas all the year, memories remain.

—

Minnie Pearl

Treasures for the Children

I assure you: Whoever does not welcome the kingdom of God like a little child will never enter it.

Luke 18:17 HCSB

hristmas is a special time for children. As the big day nears, youngsters become more and more excited. And as adults, we can learn from their excitement.

Materialism, of course, is a sign of spiritual immaturity, but joy is not. And, while our children may look longingly at brightly wrapped gifts under the tree, we adults should fix our collective gaze much higher up, at the star that symbolizes that night in Bethlehem when our Savior was born. Then, with childlike exuberance, we should encourage our children to enjoy the Christmas season while keeping them ever mindful that Christ is, and always will be, the greatest Christmas gift of all.

It is good to be children sometimes,
and never better than at Christmas,
when its mighty Founder was a child himself.

—

Charles Dickens

A child sees only delight and pleasure in the Christmas story.
So maybe part of the Christmas message is just that—
the possibility of recovering that childlike joy.

Harry Reasoner

Then He took a child, had him stand among them, and taking him in
His arms, He said to them, "Whoever welcomes one little child
such as this in My name welcomes Me. And whoever welcomes Me
does not welcome Me, but Him who sent Me."

Mark 9:36-37 HCSB

Kids go where there is excitement. They stay where there is love.

Zig Ziglar

It seems to me the secret of a joyful Christmas—especially for
children—lies in preserving not only the holiday
but also the Holy Day.

Clare Boothe Luce

Christmas is the keeping place for memories of our innocence.

Joan Mills

Every child born into the world is a new thought of God,
an ever-fresh and radiant possibility.

Kate Douglas Wiggin

*L*et the little children come to Me;
don't stop them, for the kingdom of God
belongs to such as these.

—

Mark 10:14 HCSB

*C*hildren are the hands
by which we take hold of heaven.

—

Henry Ward Beecher

Treasures from the Kitchen

They all became encouraged and took food themselves.

Acts 27:36 HCSB

During the holiday season, we indulge ourselves with
traditional food and drink, and we do so for good reason:
Our holiday feasts satisfy not only our need for sustenance
but also our need to relive the family traditions we hold dear.

The following old-time dishes are intended to tickle your taste
buds and your memories, but not necessarily in that order.

Boiled Custard

4 to 6 eggs
1 ½ c. sugar
1 T. flour
1 qt. milk
1 tsp. vanilla

Beat egg whites and yolks separately. Mix flour and sugar together and add to beaten yolks. Add beaten whites that have been beaten stiffly to yolks. Add milk to above mixture. Cook in double boiler until desired thickness. Add vanilla to cooled custard.

Christmas Eggnog

12 eggs
1 ½ c. sugar
4 ½ c. whole milk
3 c. heavy whipping cream
nutmeg

Separate the eggs. Place the egg whites in one bowl and beat until peaks form; then beat in half the sugar. In another bowl, combine the egg yolks and the other half of the sugar and beat until creamed. Combine both egg mixtures in the same bowl and beat while adding the milk. Stir in half the cream. Whip the remaining half of the cream and then fold into the mixture. Serve with nutmeg sprinkled on top of each glass.

Old-fashioned Pralines

1 lb. light brown sugar
7 to 8 T. water
1 c. pecans (more if desired)
½ stick of butter
Maple flavoring

Let sugar and water boil hard. Add pecans. Cook until mixture reaches the soft ball stage (it makes a small soft ball in ½ cup of water). Add butter and remove from heat. Beat until creamy, but of a consistency that will spread. Drop by spoonfuls onto buttered cookie sheets and let harden. Make certain there are sufficient nuts in each spoonful. For variety, try other flavorings such as chocolate, coconut, orange, etc.

Pumpkin Pie

1½ c. canned or cooked pumpkin or squash
1 c. brown sugar, firmly packed
½ tsp. salt
2 tsp. cinnamon
1 tsp. ginger
2 T. molasses
3 eggs, slightly beaten
12 oz. can of evaporated milk
1 unbaked pie shell

Preheat oven to 425°. Combine pumpkin, sugar, salt, spices, and molasses. Add eggs and milk and mix thoroughly. Pour into unbaked pie shell and bake for 40 to 45 minutes, or until knife inserted comes out clean.

Old-fashioned Sweet Potato Pie

4 med. sweet potatoes, cooked and mashed, or 1 can sweet potatoes
2 eggs
1 ½ c. sugar
1 stick butter, melted
1 tsp. vanilla
1 unbaked pie shell

Mix all ingredients well using only 1 cup sugar. Beat well and pour into 9" unbaked crust. Sprinkle ½ cup sugar evenly over the top and let pie stand for 30 minutes until sugar dissolves. Bake at 300° for 1 hour. The pie will have a crust on top.

Peanut Butter Fudge

4 c. sugar
1 c. whole milk (maybe a bit more, but not soupy)
3 to 4 heaping T. peanut butter
½ stick butter
1 T. vanilla

Mix sugar, milk, and peanut butter thoroughly with a spoon. Cook on small burner on high until the ingredients reach the soft ball stage (makes a small soft ball in ½ cup of water). The secret is to not let the mixture get too hard. Add butter and vanilla, and let cool a few minutes. Beat diligently and pour into a greased, small, elongated sheet pan. Let cool. Cut with a sharp knife.

Sugared Pecans

1 ½ c. sugar
1/3 c. water
1 tablespoon butter
2 c. of pecan halves

Combine 1½ cups sugar, 1/3 cup water, and 1 tablespoon butter. Boil until syrup will spin a thread. Pour in 2 cups of pecan halves and stir constantly until syrup begins to harden. Pour on waxed paper and separate halves and allow to cool. For variety coconut may be added to the syrup. Also try maple flavor or chocolate.

Candied Sweet Potatoes

6 medium sweet potatoes, cooked and sliced
¼ c. butter
½ c. pecans
1 c. brown sugar
¼ c. water
½ tsp. salt

Place potatoes in greased casserole. Combine remaining ingredients; pour over potatoes. Bake at 350° for 45 minutes, basting occasionally. Makes 6 servings.

Old-fashioned Chess Pie

3 eggs
½ c. butter, melted
1 ½ c. sugar
¾ tsp. vinegar
1 T. cornmeal
1 ½ tsp. vanilla
½ tsp. salt

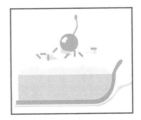

Beat the eggs and then mix in all remaining ingredients. Place the mixture in an unbaked 9-inch pie shell. Preheat the oven to 375° and bake for 15 minutes. Reduce the temperature to 350° and bake for 20-30 minutes. The pie is done when the center quivers slightly after being shaken.

And, as you enjoy these and other treasures
for the kitchen, remember the old saying,
"Enough is as good as a feast!"

Worshiping Our Savior

But an hour is coming, and is now here,
when the true worshipers will worship the Father
in spirit and truth.

John 4:23 HCSB

During this holiday season, it is proper that we keep our eyes, our voices, and our hearts lifted upward as we offer profound thanksgiving to our Creator.

When we worship God faithfully and fervently, we are blessed. When we fail to worship Him, for whatever reason, we forfeit the spiritual gifts that He intends for us.

Every day provides opportunities to put God where He belongs: at the center of our lives. Christmas Day provides a special opportunity to celebrate the birth of God's Son. When we worship Christ, not just with our words but with our deeds, we do honor to the Father, to the Son, and to ourselves.

*J*oyful, joyful, we adore Thee, God of glory, Lord of love; Hearts unfold like flowers before Thee, opening to the sun above.

—

Henry Van Dyke

To travel the road to Bethlehem is to keep a rendezvous with wonder,
to answer the call of wisdom, and to bow the knee in worship.

John A. Knight

Worship the Lord your God and . . . serve Him only.

Matthew 4:10 HCSB

The birth of Jesus is the sunrise in the Bible.

Henry Van Dyke

*G*reat little One!
whose all-embracing birth
lifts Earth to Heaven,
stoops Heaven to Earth.

—

Richard Crashaw

A Son of God who defends His title with the arguments that He is the brother of even the poorest and the guilty and takes their burden upon Himself, this is a fact one can only note and shake one's head in unbelief, or one must worship and adore. There is no other alternative. I must worship. That's why I celebrate Christmas.

Helmut Thielicke

It is impossible to worship God and remain unchanged.

Henry Blackaby

To you, O LORD, I lift up my soul. I trust in you, my God.

Psalm 25:1-2 NLT

Let us remember therefore this lesson: That to worship our God
sincerely we must evermore begin by hearkening to His voice,
and by giving ear to what He commands us. For if every man
goes after his own way, we shall wander. We may well run,
but we shall never be a whit nearer to the right way,
but rather farther away from it.

John Calvin

But be sure to fear the LORD and sincerely worship him.
Think of all the wonderful things he has done for you.

1 Samuel 12:24 HCSB

We worship in Thy holy Name;
O! bless this hour of prayer.

Fanny Crosby

Worship is an act which develops feelings for God,
not a feeling for God which is expressed in an act of worship.
When we obey the command to praise God in worship, our deep,
essential need to be in relationship with God is nurtured.

Eugene Peterson

*E*ntering the house, they saw the child
with Mary His mother, and falling
to their knees, they worshiped Him.
Then they opened their treasures
and presented Him with gifts:
gold, frankincense, and myrrh.

—

Matthew 2:11 HCSB

*L*oving Father, Help us to remember
the birth of Jesus, that we may share
in the song of the angel,
the gladness of the shepherds,
and the worship of the wise men.

—

Robert Louis Stevenson

Joy to the World

Rejoice in the Lord always. I will say it again: Rejoice!

Philippians 4:4 HCSB

C hristmas is a season of celebration and joy. It is a time when we praise God for His love and for the gift of His Son, Jesus.

Christ made it clear to His followers: He intended that His joy would become their joy. And it still holds true today: Christ intends that His believers share His love, His peace, His abundance, and His joy.

Let us accept the joy that is ours through Jesus Christ. Then, with thanksgiving in our hearts, let us gather together, like the shepherds of old, and praise the newborn babe, the humble Christ child, the Savior of the world.

*I*f you have a troubled heart,
listen to the angel's song:
"I bring you tidings of great joy!"
Jesus did not come to condemn you.
If you want to define Christ rightly,
then pay heed to how the angel defines Him:
"A great joy!"

—

Martin Luther

Joy to the World!

Joy to the world!
The Lord is come!
Let earth receive her king.

Let every heart prepare Him room,
and heaven and nature sing,
and heaven and nature sing,
and heaven, and heaven, and nature sing.

—

Isaac Watts, 1719

The light of the world is reborn in His glory
at the same season every year. Let us bless each other and be joyful.

Katherine Anne Porter

O clap your hands, all peoples;
Shout to God with the voice of joy.

Psalm 47:1 NASB

Christmas does not deny sorrow its place in the world.
But the message of Christmas is that joy is bigger than despair,
that peace will outlast turmoil, that love has crushed all the evil,
hatred, and pain that the world, at its worst, can muster.

Randall L. Frame

The old message, "For unto you is born
this day in the city of David
a Savior which is Christ the Lord,"
is still the heart of Christmas.

—

Peter Marshall

Christmas is the season of joy, of holiday greetings exchanged,
of gift-giving, and of families united.

Norman Vincent Peale

Let the hearts of those who seek the LORD rejoice.
Look to the LORD and his strength; seek his face always.

1 Chronicles 16:10-11 NIV

Joy is the great note all throughout the Bible.

Oswald Chambers

This is the day which the LORD has made;
let us rejoice and be glad in it.

—

Psalm 118:24 NASB

Rejoice, the Lord is King;
Your Lord and King adore!
Rejoice, give thanks and sing
and triumph evermore.

—

Charles Wesley

There will be joy and delight for you,
and many will rejoice at his birth.

Luke 1:14 HCSB

O the precious name of Jesus! How it thrills our souls with joy.

Lydia Baxter

My purpose is to give life in all its fullness.

John 10:10 HCSB

Floods of joy o'er my soul like
the sea billows roll,
since Jesus came into my heart.

—

Rufus H. McDaniel

Rejoice, that the immortal God is born,
so that mortal man may live in eternity.
Jan Huss

I truly believe that if we keep telling the Christmas story,
singing the Christmas songs, and living the Christmas spirit,
we can bring joy and happiness and peace to this world.
Norman Vincent Peale

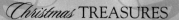

Christ and joy go together.

—

E. Stanley Jones

But the angel said to them,
"Do not be afraid, for you see,
I announce to you good news of great joy
that will be for all the people.

—

Luke 2:10 HCSB

Christmas Day is a day
of joy and charity.
May God make you
very rich in both.

—

Phillips Brooks

For God So Loved the World...

For God so loved the world that he gave his only Son,
so that everyone who believes in him will not perish
but have eternal life.

John 3:16 NLT

On the very first Christmas day, when God sent His Son to become the salvation of the world, He bestowed a gift that is beyond price and beyond human comprehension. The familiar words of John 3:16 remind us that our salvation is a blessing from God—offered freely as an outpouring of His infinite love.

All of us are imperfect; even the best among us have fallen far short of God's commandments. But, when we accept Christ into our hearts, we are saved by God's grace. This is the message and the meaning of Christmas.

During this season when we celebrate the Babe of Bethlehem, let us praise God for the gift of His Son. And then, let us share the Good News with a world that desperately needs God's priceless treasure: Jesus Christ.

To God be the glory;
great things He hath done!
So loved He the world
that He gave us his son.

—

Fanny Crosby

If we could condense all the truths of Christmas into
only three words, these would be the words: "God with us."
John MacArthur

Jesus: the proof of God's love.
Philip Yancey

Though we may not act like our Father,
there is no greater truth than this:
We are his. Unalterably. He loves us.
Undyingly. Nothing can separate us
from the love of Christ.

Max Lucado

Behold, behold the wondrous love,
That ever flows from God above
Through Christ His only Son.

Fanny Crosby

For He chose us in Him,
before the foundation of the world,
to be holy and blameless in His sight.
In love He predestined us to be adopted
through Jesus Christ for Himself,
according to His favor and will.

—

Ephesians 1:4-5 HCSB

God is a God of unconditional, unremitting love,
a love that corrects and chastens but never ceases.

Kay Arthur

Our Savior kneels down and gazes upon the darkest acts of our lives.
But rather than recoil in horror, He reaches out in kindness and says,
"I can clean that if you want." And from the basin of His grace,
He scoops a palm full of mercy and washes our sin.

Max Lucado

For the LORD your God has arrived
to live among you. He is a mighty savior.
He will rejoice over you with great gladness.
With his love, he will calm all your fears.
He will exult over you
by singing a happy song.

—

Zephaniah 3:17 HCSB

$\mathcal{L}$ove so amazing, so divine,
demands my soul,
my life, my all.

—

Isaac Watts

God's love is measureless. It is more: it is boundless.
It has no bounds because it is not a thing but a facet of
the essential nature of God. His love is something he is,
and because he is infinite, that love can enfold the whole
created world in itself and have room for ten thousand
times ten thousand worlds beside.

A. W. Tozer

The unfailing love of the LORD never ends!

Lamentations 3:22 NLT

The great love of God is an ocean
without a bottom or a shore.

—

C. H. Spurgeon

*C*hristmas, my child, is always.

—

Dale Evans

Bible Translations Used: